Tips & Tales of the Tennis Court

Published by Paige J O'Neill.

Designed by Sharon Swanbery-Forrest,
Digital Composition Services, Atlanta, Georgia.

Edited by Marti Singer and Maggie Tripp.

International Standard Book Number 0-9649392-0-7.
Printed in the United States of America.

* I have so much appreciation and love for the many people that helped make this book complete. A huge thank you to Marti Singer, Sharon Swanbery-Forrest, Maggie Tripp and Trish Dare. You know what you did to help me and I owe you!

* Thanks to Billie Jean King, Tracey Donnelly, Chris Evert, Tami Olsen, Bill Bowden, Mary Carillo, and Shannon McCarthy for your kind words.

* Thanks to many people for sharing their knowledge with me, especially Fred Romanus, Jim Haneklau, and Tori Nichols.

* Thanks to my mom and dad who invested so much time and support into my tennis career. You're the greatest!

* Thanks to all of my students over the many years for your support. I learned as much from you as I hope you learned from me.

* And thanks to my dogs, Kong and Frisko for watching me type away and never saying anything negative!

TABLE of CONTENTS

Equipment............1
Purchasing a Racket, About Balls, On Court

Rules................11
Written, Etiquette

Surviving the Weather...23
Wet, Cold, Hot

Stroke Production......29
Groundstrokes, Serves, Volleys, Overheads

Strategies.............75
Basic, Singles, Doubles, Positioning,
Return of Serve, Serve & Volley,
Poaching, Lobs, Angles, Change

Footwork............139

Mental Toughness......145

Tennisellaneous..........151

EQUIPMENT

Purchasing a Racket.........2

About Balls 6

On Court 7

Pro Shop Shopping

Visit a tennis specialty shop. Ask the tennis expert to recommend three or four rackets to hit with before you buy. (Make sure that any demo charges go towards the purchase of a racket.)

They may ask:

* Your price range. (Buy a racket that you will grow into, not out of.)
* The level of tennis you currently play.
* If you play predominantly singles and/or doubles.
* If you play mostly from the baseline or at the net.
* If you hit the ball flat or with spin.
* If you are looking for more power or more control.

Racket Head Lines

* A racket with a wider cross-section ("widebody") will generally offer more power than a narrow beam racket, which offers more control.

* A midsize racket head generally offers more control than an oversized head, which offers more power.

* The new longer rackets (up to 29" from the normal 27") are designed to add more power, more topspin, and, of course, more reach—especially on the serve.

cross-section

Get A Grip

* Grips sizes are: 4, 4⅛, 4¼, 4⅜, 4½, 4⅝.
  Generally, an average woman will use a 4¼ to a 4⅜, and an average man will use a 4⅜ to a 4⅝.

* When undecided between two sizes, buy the smaller grip size and build it up with a cushion grip or a racket grip sleeve (sold in stores).

* Reminder: If necessary, have your racket stringer also replace a worn out grip and grommet strip (plastic piece that protects the strings) .

Guts or Nylons?

* Have your racket strung the same number of times in a year that you play in a week.

* Synthetic gut strings offer power and control without the high cost of gut. However, there is a wide range of performance in synthetic strings. Ask your stringer to recommend a string for your type of game.

* String tighter for more control, looser for more power.

* String gauges range from 15 gauge (thickest) to 20 gauge (thinnest). Choose the thinnest gauge possible (typically 17) without risking frequent breakage. Hitting with heavy spin will cause strings to break more frequently.

What Balls Do I Use?

Use:

Extra duty felt balls:	Hard courts.
Regular duty balls:	Soft courts, grass courts, indoor courts.
Orange balls:	Indoor courts.
Two-tone balls:	When teaching or learning spin. Easy to identify.
Pressureless balls:	In ball machines. Longer life, buy in bulk.
White balls:	Just for nostalgia.

Open a new can of approved balls each match (check the label).
Donate old tennis balls to schools, clubs, or your favorite pets.

By the way, balls are numbered only for the purpose of identification.

Court Measurements

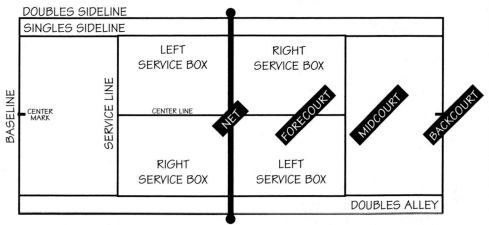

Court length=78'; Court width=36'; Alley width=4'6";
Net height=3'6"on the sides and 3' in the middle;
Net to service line distance=21'; Service line to baseline distance=18'.

Surfaces: My Pace or Yours!

Three of the most common court surfaces:

Hard Courts: A"true bounce" surface. Benefits the more powerful, harder serving player. This is the most common surface for recreational play. The *U.S. Open* and *Australian Open* are hard court venues.

Soft Courts: For a patient baseline player who is consistent, runs well and hits with spin. Drop shots and lobs are very effective and the softer surface is kinder to the body. These surfaces require maintenance (watering, rolling and brushing.) The *French Open* is played on red clay (Rubico) which is thicker and slower than the green composition (Har-Tru.)

Grass: Slickest and "least true-bouncing" surface. This surface favors the serve and volley player and the flexible player who deals well with inconsistently bouncing balls. *Wimbledon* is a grass court venue.

Wayne Penniman started his summer camps with the same group of boys that had been taking lessons for two years. Roger, a beginner, signed up half way through the camp's second session. Not only was he the smallest boy in the class, but he was quickly becoming frustrated and humiliated as he struggled just to make contact with the ball. Noticing that Roger had one of the new oversized rackets, Wayne awarded the "prize of the day" to the player who could pick up the most balls on his racket. Roger was beaming with pride when he won with 38 and his shots began to get better the very next day. Now that's a great instructor!!

RULES

Written 12

Etiquette 17

It's Your Call!

Tennis is proudly played on the honor system.

Stop the point when:

* The ball double bounces.
* Your body, clothes or racket touch the net.
* You double hit the ball intentionally (unintentional "carries" made with one motion are legal).
* The ball is first tipped by your partner.
* The ball hits any part of your body, including your racket hand.

Continue to play the point when your opponents commit any of the above. Question them after the point and remember, it's their call.

A Ball that is 99% Out...is...100% Good

Make a clear, **honest** line call!! (NOT: "Yes, I'm *pretty sure* that ball was definitely out.") Honor the proud tennis tradition of making your own calls. A ball is considered "in" if there is **any** doubt. Make line calls only on your side of the court.

The only exception for making a line call on your opponents' side is when it is in their favor. Graciously allow your partner to overrule your incorrect call, and graciously overrule them.

Never intentionally call a good ball out.

Racket, Net, Ball

It is illegal to make contact with the ball on your opponents' side of the net; however, the racket may *follow through* across the net. (Remember not to touch the net with your racket or your body.)

Exception:

A ball bounces on your side, then on its own, starts to return to the other side. You can, and must, reach over the net (without touching it) and make contact with the ball. You lose the point if you do not make contact before it bounces. This can happen on a windy day or when there is a tremendous amount of backspin on the ball.

Also, hitting around the net post is legal *and....very impressive.*

Dodge Ball

Never get hit by the opponent's ball!!!!
You lose the point if the ball hits any part of you **before** it bounces,
no matter where you are standing.

NO EXCEPTIONS!!!!!

The #2 seeded player, who was just aced by a serve, illegally left the court and demanded that Susan Norsworthy, volunteer tournament director, turn the lights on because he "couldn't see the ball". Susan refused because it was only 2:00 p.m. The next day, Susan was forced to default this same player because he was 45 minutes late. He "showed himself" again by yelling and carrying on about how unfair she was. Susan could only hold back laughter: in his haste to make his match on time, he had forgotten to pull up his zipper.

Etiquette Rules!

"Play to win,
Win without boasting,
Lose without excuse,
and...always play by the rules."

I heard this quote on a T.V. interview from a wise 99-year-old senior olympic athlete.

Pass it on!!

Tennis Etiquette, or Unwritten Rules, are Just as Important as Written Rules.

* Don't stall! The written rule states: 25 seconds between points, 90 seconds during side changes. No breaks between sets 1 and 2, 10 minutes only between sets 2 and 3. (Continuous play during tiebreaker change-overs.)
* Keep your voice down.
* Don't throw your racket or hit balls in anger.
* Don't intentionally distract an opponent.
* Speak nicely to your opponent.
* Don't start serving until you have two balls available.
* Wait for a point to be completed before walking behind a court.
* Close the gate behind you when entering or leaving the court. (This keeps the flies out.)

Shake! Shake! Shake!

Give a firm handshake
with eye contact at the
end of the match.

Watch Your Watching!

❋ Applaud only when a good shot has been hit or a good point has been played.

❋ **Do not** applaud an unforced error, such as a double fault.

❋ By the way, save some food, drink, and ice for the players who are last off the court. **Thanks!**

Laura Jeu de Vine was having a difficult time concentrating on her match because of the side show on the next court. A college player with a really bad attitude broke a string in his favorite racket. He sent his second racket airborne, high into the tree tops where it hooked a limb and never fell to the ground. When he broke a string in his third racket, he had to default the match...No one would lend him a fourth.

SURVIVING
the
WEATHER

Wet 24

Cold 25

Hot 26

Quick-Dry Method

Squeegee wet courts in one continuous circular motion,
starting at the "T".

Common Cold Cures

In cold weather:

* Remove all jewelry, especially earrings.
* Wear several layers of clothing.
* Warm up with easy hitting or a brief jog, then do some stretching exercises.
* Never stretch cold muscles.
* Cover your ears with a warm hat or ear muffs.
* Bundle up immediately after play is over.

Beat the Heat!

Sunglasses - Make a long-term investment in your eyes:

* Wear high quality sunglasses offering 100% protection from all harmful rays of the sun.
* Use a lens that is single gradient (all one color).
* Select a durable frame and use a sunglass retainer to prevent your sunglasses from hitting the ground.
* Some companies offer unconditional one year warranties...remember that for your next purchase.

Sunscreen - A fair-skinned person can sunburn within 10 minutes; anyone can burn after three hours on the court:

* Wear a non-greasy, rubproof and sweatproof sunscreen on your face, legs and arms.
* Remember to protect your lips, nose, ears, shoulders and knees.
* Use a roll-up stick so you can apply it hands free.
* Keep plenty of sunscreen available in your tennis bag, and USE IT.
* A sunless tanning lotion will get rid of those truly attractive tennis sock lines.

Wear a hat!

Socks

* Wear acrylic socks to "wick" perspiration away from your feet.
* Tennis-specific socks are padded in the heels and the balls of your feet and have less padding in the arch.
* High quality socks will last longer and will be healthier for your feet by preventing friction that causes blistering.

Shoes

* Wear a pair of shoes with a good inner cushioning design.
* Any tennis shoe tread offers good traction for hard courts.
* Herringbone tread pattern is most popular to wear on clay courts.
* Grass court shoes have spikes for added traction.

Don't skimp here!

Think Drink

Sports drinks replenish carbohydrates, sugars, sodium, potassium, and chlorides. Drink plenty of water the night before a match but drink a sports drink before, during, and after a particularly tough match or in extremely hot weather. Sports drinks can actually improve your performance by replacing glycogen, which will prevent muscle fatigue.

STROKE PRODUCTION

Groundstrokes 30

Serves 50

Volleys 62

Overheads 72

Grab a Grip

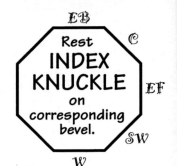

View of Racket Butt

EF EASTERN FOREHAND: "Shake hands".
A basic grip used for modified topspin.

EB EASTERN BACKHAND: For a one-handed or two-handed backhand. A basic grip used for modified topspin.

C CONTINENTAL: "Hammer". Used for volleys (forehand & backhand), serves, overheads, two-handed backhands and when hitting with underspin.

SW SEMI-WESTERN FOREHAND: Between Continental & Western. Used for heavy topspin.

W WESTERN FOREHAND: "Underhand frying pan". Use for extreme topspin.

Change your grip to change the angle of your strings.

More Placement...Less Power

Practice groundstrokes (and all strokes) in this order:

* Consistency
* Direction
* Depth
* Spin
* Power

Not this order:

* Power
* Power
* Power

At Andy Durham's junior boys indoor tournament at Kingsbury Club in Kingsbury, MA, the atmosphere was becoming more and more intense. Eight singles players battled for points on four courts. The parents watched nervously from behind the glass-enclosed loft. Suddenly, a squirrel appeared on Court 1. The two boys stopped playing and chased it onto Court 2 where play was once again suspended and the four boys chased it onto Court 3. From Court 3, six boys chased the poor squirrel onto Court 4, and the parents watched in amazement as the eight boys, now armed with rackets, racket covers, bags, towels, and trash cans, pursued the rascal with the same ferociousness as they had faced each other on court. The entire complex cheered when the victors formed a circle around the squirrel and walked it outside to freedom. The kids never knew competition could be so much fun!!

Racket Back & Down

❋ Complete your backswing before the ball bounces.

❋ Increase the amount of topspin on the ball by looping the backswing.
 This will also help your timing, especially when playing against off-pace hitters.

Contact Point

Contact the ball just in front of your forward foot.

 Point of Contact

Forward Foot

Swing Low to High

"Arc" the ball over the net with modified topspin to increase consistency and depth of groundstrokes.

Follow Through "On Edge"

The edge of your racket should be perpendicular to the ground.

"Hey Batter, Batter...SWING!"

Force your opponents to hit out of **their** strike zones by hitting:

* "Low", below the knees.

* "High", above the shoulders.

* "On the run", away from the body.

* "Tight", in close to the body.

*Use good footwork to position yourself
to contact the ball within your strike zone.*

Pam was taking a private lesson from Juan, the drop-dead gorgeous, new-to-the-area, tennis pro. During the lesson she heard him instruct, "Aye neid tu' see yore knockers." She thought she misunderstood him until she heard it again, "Aye neid tu' see yore knockers." Slightly embarrassed, she confronted him by asking, "Juan, what are you saying? Do you need to see my chest on the follow-through?" "No, I neid tu see yore K N U C K L E S." (on the follow-through). To this day, Pam's knuckles are clearly visible on *every* follow-through!

Put Your Non-Racket Hand to Work

Right handers, point your left hand at an on-coming ball to:

* Establish a hitting ("strike") zone.

* Turn your shoulders.

* Contact the ball early.

* Catch the racket with your left hand during the follow-through.

Sorry lefties, think opposite on the next few pages...

"How Many Forehands Do You Have?"

Most players have good backswings and good contact points, but a hundred different follow-throughs.

Develop a *consistent* follow-through and promise, promise, promise to use it on every stroke possible!

☆One-Handed Backhand

Change your grip to the Eastern Backhand.
(See page 30.) This will prevent your strings
from "opening" which can cause the ball to
go out.

Put index knuckle here on top.

Eastern
Backhand Grip

(Racket Butt)

4 Steps to a Better Backswing

For a One-Handed Backhand:

* "Pull" the racket back with your non-racket hand.

* Change your grip during the backswing.

* Point the back of your right shoulder (left shoulder for lefties) directly at the on-coming ball.

* Touch your racket hand "thumb to thigh".

Swing Low to High, Stop at the Sky

Start your swing by pointing your racket toward the ground behind you. Swing forward and up to contact the ball. Finish the stroke by pointing the racket toward the sky on your follow-through.

Full Wingspan

* Leave your non-racket hand behind you as you follow through to prevent shoulder rotation.

* You should look like an eagle soaring with a full wingspan!!!

Two-Handed Backhand

Turn a defensive "just get it over" one-handed backhand into an offensive booming weapon:

❋ Use an eastern forehand grip for your left hand.

❋ Change the grip of your right hand to whichever is more comfortable—
eastern forehand, eastern backhand, or continental grip.

Accelerate, Don't Brake

Use your left arm as an accelerator, not as a brake when hitting two-handed backhands.

Have some fun while you practice your follow-through:

* Hold your racket in your left hand.
* Concentrate on stroking low to high with the follow-through finishing "on edge" between your shoulder blades.
* Then add your right hand.

"Thumb to Thigh"

For both one-handed and two-handed backhands, remembering "thumb to thigh" or "pick pocket" on your backswing will:

* Keep your hands in close to your body.

* Keep your elbow straight, but not locked.

* Keep your racket low.

Point of Contact

The contact point of a two-handed backhand
is slightly later than a one-handed backhand.

⊚

Weight Shift

Bend your front knee to shift your weight forward.

*Now you will be like a "switch hitter" in baseball,....
a strong hitter on both sides.*

Little Sarah Harrison and Sara Bennett had their third beginner tennis lesson with their 32-year-old instructor, Marty Kunsman. After the lesson, Carla Harrison asked her daughter what she thought of her new tennis pro. Sarah cooed, "Ohhhh mom...I'm going to marry him when I grow up." At that remark, Sara Bennett snorted, "He'll be dead by the time you grow up!" Youth!!

The 3-Part Serve

1. BACKSWING - Get your elbow in a throwing position. (Behind you and up.)
2. CONTACT POINT - Swing "up" to the ball.
3. FOLLOW THROUGH - Swing across your body to complete your stroke.

If you do not have a good backswing, you will not have a good contact point. If you do not have a good contact point, you will not have a good follow-through. Work on 1, *then* 2, *then* 3.

Toss & Catch, Toss & Bounce, Toss & Hit

Practice toss and:

* CATCH: The ball should fall directly into your extended left hand.

* BOUNCE: Bounce the toss (instead of hitting it).

  1. For a flat serve the toss should bounce inside the baseline and to the right of your forward foot.
  2. For a slice, the toss should bounce just inside the baseline to the right of your body.
  3. For a topspin, the toss should bounce on top of your head.

* HIT: Go for it!

Emphasize the AND for better timing on the serve. It's not "toss/hit", it's "toss AND hit".

"Brush" the Ball in an Upward Motion

Brushing the ball:

* Increases the net clearance which adds consistency and depth.

* Adds modified or heavy spin.

* Adds pace because of increased racket action.

Visualize the ball going "up" off of your racket, not down!

Follow-Through "☆n Edge"

A correct follow-through forces the racket to swing properly.
Finish so the edge of your racket brushes past the outside of your left leg
(right leg for lefties).

☆uch!

Don't hit yourself!

Losing Your Service Games?

* **Observe your Serve:** Increase the percentage of your first serves. Change the placement of your serve.
* **Reposition your Partner:** Closer to the net, closer to the service line, back to the baseline, or into the *Australian* doubles positions.
* **Reposition Yourself:** Stand closer to the alley to add more angle to your serve; or, move closer to the center line to take the angle off.
* **Reposition yourself AFTER serving:** Serve and volley, serve and stay back, or serve and half-volley (pick the ball up immediately off the bounce).

Stand Closer to the Center Line

Standing close to the center line when serving from the deuce side (right) will:

* Make it easier to place the ball down the middle of the service box or near the center line.
* Help you serve into the body of your opponent.
* Allow you to hit more forehands.
* Keep the middle of your court tight.
* Make it easier to run down lobs.
* Better position you to serve and volley.

Use this position in singles as well as doubles.

Stand Closer to the Alley

Standing close to the alley when serving from the ad side (left) in doubles will:

* Make it easier to serve to the opponent's backhand.

* Help to hit a wide serve and open the opponents' middle.

* Allow you to hit more forehands protecting a weaker backhand.

In singles, stand closer to the center line when serving.

Change your stance whenever necessary.

Get Your First Serve in Play!

FIRST SERVE...
ADVANTAGE SERVER

SECOND SERVE...
ADVANTAGE RETURNER

GET YOUR FIRST SERVE IN PLAY!
GET YOUR FIRST SERVE IN PLAY!
GET YOUR FIRST SERVE IN PLAY!
GET YOUR FIRST SERVE IN PLAY!
GET YOUR FIRST SERVE IN PLAY!
GET YOUR FIRST SERVE IN PLAY!
GET YOUR FIRST SERVE IN PLAY!
GET YOUR FIRST SERVE IN PLAY!

Seek & You Shall Find

In the warm-up and early in the match:

* Check out your opponent's backhand. Remember, a few players, **and most lefties,** like their backhands better than their forehands.
* Try to find out if they have trouble returning off-pace serves, high bouncing serves, and/or spin serves.

Don't have a spin serve? Learn one!

Still Unsure Where to Serve?

Serve into the returner's body when you are not sure where to serve.

⊙

Center Line Set-Up

Set up your partner for a poach by serving down the center line.

Change Your Serves as a Baseball Pitcher Changes the Pitch

Vary the serve by adjusting:

* Pace
* Depth
* Spin
* Height
* Placement
* Angle

Sydney Carrick was playing a high school tennis match against a less experienced player. Serving the first point of the match, Sydney aced her opponent. She repeated with an ace on the second point. Her opponent swung and totally whiffed the third point, making it 40-love. Sydney's next serve was so strong that her opponent could only react by catching the ball as it spun her way. "That's it, I quit," said her opponent. She shook Sydney's hand and that three-minute match was history.

Move In!

Moving in to volley the ball:

* Gives opponent less time to react.

* Keeps you and your partner on the net (offense).

* Keeps your opponent off of the net (defense).

* Pressures the opponent to hit shots they don't have.

Play a practice match with a "no bounce" rule: If the ball bounces behind your service line you lose the point. This will force you to move in and volley every shot, lobs included. The ball is allowed to bounce within the service boxes.

Ready? Prepare to Volley!

Ready position for the volley:

* Feet shoulder-width apart, knees bent, weight forward.

* Continental, "hammer" grip.

* Left hand lightly grips throat of racket.

* Elbows in front and in tight to your body.
  (Keeping your right elbow in close to
  your belly button, try taking your racket
  behind you. Can't do it, can you?)

* Racket head shoulder level.

How Low Can It Go?

Check the height of the bounce of your volley.

Does it bounce up?

Boo!

Or...

Does it stay low?

Yea!

Open String Volley

Volley the ball with slightly open strings. This will add underspin, which will:

* Lift the ball ***up*** over the net.

* Add depth.

* Keep the bounce low.

* Give you more ball control.

Warning: Keep the racket head up. Dropping the racket head will cause you to contact the bottom of the ball and hit it out.

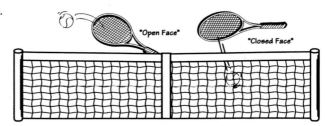

Low Volleys - In Play
High Volleys - Put Away!

When you are forced to hit a low volley (below the waist),
put it "in play" deep.
"Put away" a high volley with power or touch.

Put Away Your Put-Aways!

To keep your offensive (winning) volley from coming back:

* Hit to the closest player's side of the court. He has less time to react.

* Hit with depth or angle to prevent the ball from bouncing in front of your opponent.

* Close the net. It's difficult to hit winners from the service line.

"Handcuff" Your Hands Together for a Better Contact Point

It's impossible to take a backswing
if your hands are close together.

A Good Volley Never Bounces in the Service Box

Hit the ball either deep or with angle.
(Unless you are hitting a drop volley, of course!)

Learn a "Drop" Volley!

a.k.a.:
* "Touch" volley
* "Bunt" volley
* "Loose grip" volley
* "Raw egg" volley. (Don't crack it!)

Get the picture?

A successful drop volley or drop shot will bounce at least three times ***inside*** the service box.

Peter Howell had a new adult-beginner student. To develop confidence immediatly, Peter put her close to the net and fed high, soft balls for her to volley. She totally whiffed every shot, however, because of a persistent, unorthodox wrist motion. Peter tried everything! He moved in closer, he hit higher, he even threw the balls at her racket, but she continued to miss. After several baskets of balls, Peter explained, "Tennis is a tough sport and not necessarily for everyone. Why is it so important for you to learn tennis?" he asked. "Everyone I know quit the bridge club and took up tennis when Billie Jean King beat that Riggs man," she answered.

Lesson number two started and ended the same way. During lesson number three, Peter finally stopped, walked over to her and asked, "Have you ever considered learning golf?" She began to cry, and said, "The golf pro sent me **to you**."

Her perserverance paid off. One year later she was given an award from her B team as the player who "looks the worst, but plays the best!"

Prepare Quickly for An Overhead

* Turn sideways.
* Racket behind your head. Keep your hitting hand next to your ear.
* Non-racket hand points to the ball.
* Adjust your steps.
* Weight on back foot.
* Then swing with confidence! Go to the ball, don't wait for the ball to come to you.

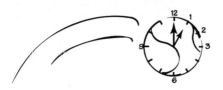

Overhead Wisdom

* Contact the ball as high as you can, at "Twelve" or "One" O'Clock.
* Close the net behind an overhead to prevent the next ball from hitting your feet.
* Swing confidently when hitting an overhead! This is an offensive shot.

Go for it!

Pricilla, a.k.a "Rilla", was in the middle of a great match. As her teammates completed their own matches, they pulled up a chair to watch Rilla. The match was in a third set and things were getting intense. Her teammates rooted her on.... "GO! GO! GO! GO RILLA". "GO! GO! GO! GORILLA!!"

STRATEGIES

Basic Strategy 77

Singles. 96

Doubles 101

Positioning 105

Return of Serve. 112

Serve & Volley 118

Poaching. 122

Lobs 127

Angles. 132

Change 134

Lee Myers-Brandt was coaching an 8-year-old boys' tennis team. At practice they all fought to be the one to officially start a match by spinning their rackets. Whoever won the serve relished holding the balls and commanding the attention of the court while announcing,"Love-Love, First Serve!" Then, one day at practice, Lee heard a new announcement, "Love-Love, FBI!" (FBI means the First Ball In---on the serve---will be the one that starts the match.) One of the players had picked up this new service lingo and had everyone using it. Well, at an actual match a few weeks later, young Brian, who had not quite grasped the "First Ball In" concept, used a new version of it. As the **receiver**, Brian shouted "FBI" to the server who nodded and proceeded to put his serve in play. Brian netted the ball and returned to his original position. "Did I not just win that point?" the server asked. "No," Brian responded, "We are playing FBI, remember?" "Oh yeah, sorry, I forgot" said the server. Looking a bit puzzled, he proceeded to serve again. Eight serves and two double faults later, the return was put in play, and the match began.

Win the Spin?

Choices:

1. Serve First: a. Confident in your serves.
   b. Strong partner at the net.
2. Receive First: a. Confident in your returns.
   b. Notice your opponent(s) have weak serves.
   c. Slow to warm up.
3. Specific Side: a. Sun or wind advantage.
   b. Background distraction.

Wait... you have one more choice!

4. Let your opponent choose to serve or receive; this allows you to choose the side you want when you have a dominant server **and** the side matters.

Play the Ball, Not the Opponent!

Do not be intimidated by your opponents if they have a reputation (good or bad), if they are taller (or more muscular), if they are older (or younger), or even pregnant (okay, now you're in trouble).

Do You Get My Point?

There are only TWO ways to win a point:
1. Hit a winner.
2. Opponent's error.

Figure out a way to get your opponent to make more errors!

To Err is Human

Force your opponents to error by:

* Keeping the ball in play.

* Hitting to their weakness (forehand vs. backhand.)

* Hitting to the weaker player.

* Changing the pace. (Harder hitters thrive on pace.)

* Adding spin.

* Varying the height of the ball.

* Repositioning them. (Move baseliners in, net players back.)

* Forcing them to hit on the run.

* Forcing them to hit more low percentage shots.

* Threatening to poach.

Which of these would force you to hit more errors?

Traffic Light Strategy

Backcourt: "Green light" = Keep the ball in play (keep the traffic moving!)
Midcourt: "Yellow light" = Set yourself up and move in (clear the intersection!) This is the most difficult zone to play.
Forecourt: "Red light" = Put the ball away (stop the point!)

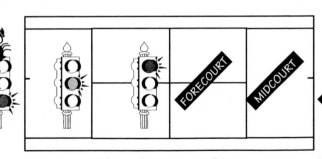

Hit from green light to green light.
Hit from yellow light to yellow or green light.
Hit from red light to red, yellow, or green light.

Troubleshoot Your Traffic Light

1. Hitting too many unforced errors? You may be:
a. Using red light strategy from green or yellow light territory.
b. Hitting from green light to red light (low percentage shot).
c. Playing the point from yellow light and not closing to red.

2. Getting lobbed too often when your playing the net? You may be:
a. Hitting from red light to green light player.
b. Moving into red light behind a weak shot.
c. Using green-light strategy from red-light territory.

Lights Out!

* Identify if your opponent likes to play from green-light, yellow-light or red-light territory. Then move them **out** of there. Reposition them into a territory where they are less comfortable and will hit more errors.

* Bring a green-light player (baseliner) in to the yellow-light area by hitting short, low balls.

* Move an aggressive red-light player to the yellow-light area by hitting a few lobs.

Stay ☆Out of "No Man's Land"

* "No man's land" is between the baseline and the service line.
* It is okay to hit **one** shot from there, but immediately move in or get back.
* Hit deep to an opponent who stands in "no man's land".

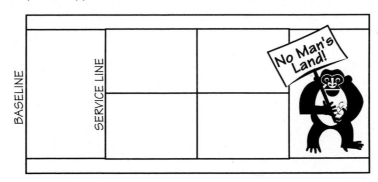

Forewards...Not Backwards

Rarely should you move backwards from yellow light to green light. However, you **should** move backwards during a point in these two situations:

When:
1. Your opponent is setting up for an overhead.
2. You are chasing a lob.

If you choose to play from the baseline in doubles, position yourself there **before** the point is in play.

Volleyball Strategy

BASELINE PLAYER: Keeps the ball "in play".
MID-COURT PLAYER: "Sets up" the point for the net player.
NET PLAYER: "Spikes" (volleys/overheads) the ball away.

Do you ever see the baseliner in volleyball try to put the ball away? If so, the net player better duck!

LOW, you GO!
HIGH, you DIE!

Move in when you hit the ball low,
duck when you hit the ball high.

Chip and Charge

Hit a chip (underspin) to keep the bounce of the ball low and slow.

This forces your opponent to hit "up" on a low ball making an easy put-away volley.

Don't forget to charge!

Be Middle-Minded

A ball hit down the middle:

* Usually is returned back down the middle, setting up your partner to poach.
* Reduces the amount of angle from your opponent, which allows you to cover less of your court.
* Keeps unforced errors at a minimum by staying away from the sidelines.
* Travels over the lowest part of the net. (Net clearance is 6" lower.)
* Often causes confusion for the opposing doubles team.

The Choice Is Yours

* When you hit to your opponents' strengths, you play against their strongest shots.

* When you hit to your opponents' weaknesses, you play against their weakest shots.

Well ????

"Prevention" Is the Best Medicine

* Hit angles and short balls against a lobber.

* Hit deeper against a player who loves to angle.

* Serve towards the center line against a player who likes to return down the alley.

Don't think..."How can I run faster to get that stupid lob?"
Think..."How can I prevent my opponent from hitting that stupid lob?"

Play According to the Score!

Use "HIGH" percentage shots on crucial points (30-15, ad, deuce, tiebreaker, etc).

Use "HIGH" or "LOW" percentage shots on non-crucial points.

HIGH percentage shots:
1. Crosscourt
2. Down the middle
3. Lobs

LOW percentage shots:
1. Down the alley
2. Angles
3. Drop shots

When serving on a crucial point, think "FIRST serve in".
When returning, think "return of serve IN PLAY".

30-15: The "Turning Point" Point

This is the most important score of the game! Use high percentage shots only! No unforced errors! In other words, don't try any hot dog shots!!

* When winning 30-15, fight for this point to make the score 40-15 vs 30-30. Or,
* When losing 30-15, fight for this point to make the score 30-30, instead of being down 40-15.

Likewise, consider 4-3 in games (or 3-4) the turning point of a set.

Tiebreaker Tidbits

* A tiebreaker is played when the set score is 6-6.
* ***Relax!***
* Think middle! High percentage!
* Win the first point!
* When you are winning, quicken the pace. When you are losing, slow the pace.
* Continuous play on change-overs. You are not allowed to sit.
* A tiebreaker is recorded as: set score (tiebreaker score). For example: 7-6(7-2).
* Take the 10-minute break if you lose a second-set tiebreaker.
* Change sides of the court to start a new set.
* The team that did ***not*** serve first in the tiebreaker, serves first in the new set.
* Win the first game of the new set.

Sharon Swanbery-Forrest, playing AA mixed doubles, was partnered with Spanish speaking Thomas (pronounced To MAS') for the first time. They were playing extremely well together; however, Sharon noticed whenever Thomas hit a ball into the net he would yell "VEG TA BULL". Sharon was stumped. She finally asked him why he was yelling vegetable. He replied with a chuckle, "noh, noh, Aye em saying 'vatch z bel' (watch the ball)!"

Win with Topspin

Use topspin groundstrokes from the baseline to:

* Add consistency and reduce the number of unforced errors. (Topspin produces higher net clearance).
* Make it difficult for your opponent to attack. (Topspin keeps the ball deep).
* Force your opponent to hit out of his strike zone. (Topspin produces a higher bounce).

Use topspin as an offensive weapon on short high balls.

Shot Selection

* **Hit crosscourt** from the baseline at the beginning of your match. It's the highest percentage shot using the lowest part of the net (6" lower). Also hit crosscourt when you are off balance and need time to recover.

* **Hit down the line** when you move inside the baseline. This gives your opponent less time to react, and no angle to play with.

* **Hit down the middle** when you want to keep your opponent from hitting angles.

Be patient!

Keep the ball in play until your opponent errors,
or until you find the right opportunity to hit your offensive shot.

"Approach" Shots

WHO hits Approach Shots?

You should move in behind good shots. Keep the ball deeper against a player who likes to move in.

WHAT is an Approach Shot?

A shot that you follow in to the net after hitting.

WHEN do I hit an Approach Shot?

Approach off of an opponent's weak shot, your strong shot, when your opponent is off balance, or when you need to play offensive tennis.

WHY should I approach?

A good approach shot (deep, low, to their weakness) will set up a weak return for you to hit a winning volley or overhead. Moving in behind a weak approach shot (short, high, to their strength) will only get you lobbed over, passed, or hit at the net.

HOW do I approach?

Approach in straight lines. Hit from the middle of the court, to the middle of the court. Hit a crosscourt shot down the line.

Don't Get Passed Up

Move in closer to the net in singles to prevent getting passed.
Always watch for those nasty lobs.

Scott was unusually lethargic throughout his private one-hour lesson. After the lesson was over, I asked the 10-year-old to kindly take my two hoppers of balls to my car. He responded in his lazy, lethargic way, "I don't reeeeally waaaant toooo." I said, "Never mind, Scott, I'll do it. I'm a female and I'm stronger". Immediately, he lifted his head high, grabbed my baskets and started towards my car. "My goodness, Scott", I said, "Do you have a male ego?" "No", he responded. "But I have two cats and a dog!"

Jumping Jack Pact

* Your number-one goal as a doubles team is to keep a tight middle! (Stay away from the alleys, think poach, and force your opponents to hit winners to the outside of your court.)

* Equally important is to open your opponents' middle. (Hit down the alley early in the match to prevent poaching, use lobs and angles.)

Whenever a winner is hit through your middle (in practice),
BOTH players do ten jumping jacks.
(Actually, you should do sit-ups to tighten YOUR middle!)

Begin Aggressively in Doubles

* Serve and volley.
* Poach.
* Attack short balls.
* Close behind return of serves.
* Change your strategy to be less aggressive if necessary.

Let's Chat!

Communicate with your partner about:

* Opponents' strengths and weaknesses.

* Your strategy on return of serves.

* Your strategy on serve placement.

* Poaching.

* Your opponents' positioning; your own positioning.

* And of course, whether your opponents are lefties.

Remember, you are allowed only 25 seconds between points.

An Invitation to My Opponent

Dear Mya Ponent: I invite you to hit down my alley in this match. You may pass me a few times and even though it's a wee bit embarrassing, I will continue to leave it open. When you prove to me that you can make the shot 60% of the time, then I will consider covering it. Remember, if you only make it 40% of the time, I will be ahead. Thanks and good luck.

Ima Gonnawin

Dear Ima Gonnawin: Thanks for the invite. Even though I know I can hit down the alley, I prefer to hit everything crosscourt. I would appreciate it if you would cover your alley and leave the rest of the court open. Thanks and good luck.

Mya Ponent

Don't Stand by Your Partner

When both players are at the net, use the split position
(one player closer to the net than the other),
instead of side by side. This strategy:

* Keeps the middle tighter.
* Allows players to stay aggressive
  towards the middle.
* Better positions you to run down a lob.
* And, best of all, will prevent you from
  getting in each other's way.

Leslie Schoeplein and Erin Deere, from Chestnut Grove Subdivision, were in the first game of their doubles match. Ten-year-old Leslie retrieved the ball she had just hit into the bottom of the net. When Leslie's hand touched the net, her opponent explained , "You are **never** allowed to touch the net," and proceeded to give herself a point. The parents kept their comments to themselves but enjoyed watching the girls meticulously pick the balls out of the net for the entire match, making sure not to touch it with their hands or their rackets. Where's the video camera when you need it?

Server's Partner

Goals:
* ***Never stop moving!!***
* Put the ball away.
* Intimidate your opponent into hitting errors on the return of serve.

It is possible to be a fantastic net player and never even hit a ball.

Middle of the Road...
I Mean... Box

Start your match standing directly in the middle of your box or as close to the center line as possible, then....

* Move closer to the net against a returner who hits low, and/or hits with angle, and is a weak lobber.

* Move closer to the service line against an opponent who hits high.

* Move to the alley ***during the point*** only when you anticipate a down-the-alley shot.

Returner's Partner

a.k.a.: "HOT SEAT" PLAYER

Goals:

* Call the serve "out" when it bounces behind the service line. Let your partner (the returner) call the center line and the alley line.
* Watch the opposing net player once the serve bounces good. (Don't watch your partner hit.)
* Defend the middle of your court! Force the net player to volley to the outside of your court to increase their unforced errors.

P.S. Don't get hit by the serve (before the bounce), or you lose the point!

Defense First

The hot seat is a defensive position covering the middle of your court.

Stand in the hot seat when your partner is returning serve, then...
* "Move in" only when your partner returns a good shot
  (deep, low, angled or away from the net player.)
* "Stay" in the hot seat when your partner returns a weak shot
  (short, high, or to the net player).

Follow the Bouncing Ball

Move ***within your service box*** according to where the ball is on the court.

Nine-year-old identical twins, Shannon and Shawn McCarthy entered their first doubles tennis tournament. Their winning strategy? Shannon, the better server, decided that she would serve the entire match and let Shawn, the better returner, return every serve. Because they were identical and were both wearing the tournament T-shirts, the only one to notice the illegal act was their mother, Andi. Knowing it was illegal to say anything, Andi impatiently waited for the match to end (in victory) to discuss the problem. They learned quickly......and went on to play #1 and #2 at the University of Georgia.

5 Returns To Know

Higher percentage:

* Crosscourt - most consistent.
* Down the middle - sets partner up for poach.
* Lob down the line - forces opponents to run, moves net player back.

Lower percentage:

* Short angle - forces opponents to run.
* Down the alley - keeps net player from poaching, opens opponents' middle.

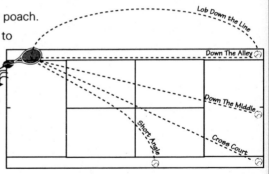

$$URS = DF$$

* An unforced error on the return of serve (URS) is just as damaging as a server's double fault (DF).
* When you fail to put the ball in play, you have 0% (NADA!) chance of winning the point.
* Don't fret about an opponent's great serve. They cause "forced errors", not "unforced errors".

"Return" Means RETURN!

Goals of the Return of Serve:
　✳ Get the ball in play!
　✳ Hit to the opponents' weaknesses.

Be Serious Now

Use high percentage crosscourt, down the middle, or lob returns on these crucial points:

* Deuce points.

* Ad points.

* 30-15, or 15-30 (most important score of the game).

* Tiebreaker points.

* Game, set, and match points.

I.⊛.U.

* Trying to hit winners on the return of serve only leads to increased unforced errors.
* Owe your partner a quarter (or a drink) for every unforced error you hit on the return of serve. (And he owes you, too.)

Move Back to Return Hard Serves, Move Up to Return Spin Serves

Lisa McManus, a true southern sweetheart, was teaching a group of
10-and-under girls how to keep score. Because of Lisa's adorable
accent, they all understood the score to be 15-Y'all, instead of 15-All.

Serve & Volley

WHEN?
* At the beginning of your match.
* Against angled returns.
* Against short returns.
* Against deep returns.
* To change your strategy.

WHEN NOT TO?
* Against good lobbers.
* Against low returns.
* When you are having a very bad day.

Don't forget, you can also serve and half volley by moving just inside of the baseline after serving. Use this when the returner hits short and low.

Most Likely to Succeed

Serve and volley with success when you:

* Get your first serve in!!

* Take your time! Don't try to get in too far, too fast.

* Stop! Split step before reaching the service line or just as the returner is ready to make contact with the ball.

* Think first volley "in play" (not "put away")! Only when the return is high do you have permission to think "winner".

* Low, you go! Move in further behind a good offensive volley (low, angled, deep, etc.). Don't move in if you hit a short high ball.

Pace Can Hurt

When serving and volleying, hit a deep, ¾-pace serve.

A fast serve may work against you because:

* You have less time to move into position.
* The return of serve will come back just as fast,
  (if not faster).
* You will have a hot volley to handle with less time to react.

Coach Jacque Green's 10-and-under team ventured off to play its first away match. When they returned, Jacque asked the boys how they did. They said, "Fine, but the other team kept yelling 'footballs' every time we served." Jacque repressed a giggle and gave them a half-hour lesson on how to serve without "footfaulting."

Coach Says Poach - "Forward!"

Move forward, towards the center strap on the net to:

* Put the ball away (instead of keeping it in play)!
* Avoid taking your partner's head off.
* Cut off opponent's angle.

Train Yourself and Your Partner

Take advantage of weak returns caused by your partner's strong serves.

Poach on a serve that is:
* Deep.
* Down the center line.
* To the returner's weakness.
* Into the returner's body.
* Tempting enough for you.

Poach *during* the point as well as on the return of serve. If you are not getting passed down your alley at least once a game, you are not doing your job.

If your partner is not poaching when you are setting him up, get the whip!

Preplan a Poach, or, Poach Instinctively

Fake a poach, even when you don't plan to poach.

'❻'

Bbbbut...When Ddddo I Ggggo?

Start to poach when your opponent drops his eyes to start his swing.
Fake a poach when your opponent's head is up, **before** he starts his swing.

Don't Avoid.....ATTACK!

Instead of trying to hit around a good net player, hit towards him early in the match.

* Return serves down his alley.
* Hit down his alley during the point.
* Lob over his head to move him off of the net.
* Hit directly at him. Chances are he will be moving and will not be in that spot once the ball is put in play.

After completing several drills, Steve Lottinger had his ladies play some games. One partnership consisted of the smallest woman in the class and the **largest** woman (and he meant large!). Set up to serve the ball, wee little Tina politely asked Mary to move over so she wouldn't hit her. "Just serve," said Mary, filling the whole court with her very intimidating ready position. So Tina served, hitting Mary square in the "cheeks". As Mary jerked straight up, the ball "caught" somewhere under her skirt. Total silence fell over the court as in a panic, Mary dropped her racket and frantically searched for the lost ball. Not until after Mary had found the ball did she start to laugh. Then everyone, including Steve, lost it.

Get Your Opponents Off Balance
...then, KEEP Them Off Balance!

* Move in, only to the service line, behind a good lob that makes your opponents run. Even though they will probably lob the return, anticipate it to be weak and prepare to move in further to hit your winner. If they hit a deep lob, you can quickly get to it and put it in play.

* Move in closer to the net when you anticipate your opponent returning your lob with a drive.

* When you are off balance, hit a high lob (defensive) to allow you recovery time.

Lob That Pesky Net Player

* Aggressive net players tend to stand very close to the net, making it very easy to lob over their heads. This strategy also forces your opponents off balance because the server must run to the ball.

* The ball travels slowly through the air on a lob. Limit your backswing and fol low-through as if you are in slow motion. For a lob with more pace, use topspin.

* Once the net player moves back a few steps, hit down the middle of the court.

Lob a Net Player, Drive a Service Line Player.

To run down a lob that is hit well over your head, turn your back towards the net, run to the center mark and circle behind the ball. Your goal is to beat the ball back to the baseline. This will give you time to find the ball later.

Gotta run!

Defense Against Good Lobbers

* Reposition them. Bring them into the net by using angles and short balls.
* Hit to their weaker sides. Most players lob better from the forehand side.
* Hit higher lobs to them for a while.
* As a last resort, volley their lobs in the air from "no man's land."
  Then move in when you hit a good shot.
* If this doesn't work...You are on your own!

My "Complements"!

Angles and lobs complement each other:

* Lob the ball when your opponent moves in for your angles.

* Angle the ball when your opponent moves back for your lobs.

"Touch" Your Angles

* Treat the ball as if it were a raw egg.

* Use the width of the court for angles (36 feet), use the length of the court for harder hit shots (78 feet).

Strings to Your Target!

The ball will travel in the direction that your strings are pointed when you make contact with the ball.

The closer you are to the net, the sharper the angle you can hit.

Dee Ann Hansel was teaching a group of kids how to keep score. She explained "deuce", then asked if anyone knew what "advantage in" was. "Well of course", one student replied, "That's a hotel in Florida". Then Dee Ann asked a promising young player if she would be interested in playing singles in the line-up. She replied, "Only if you will tell me who my partner is".

40-Love and 7 Games Ago, I was Winning this Match

Position yourself at the baseline and move in during the point when:

* The momentum has swung in favor of your opponents.

  Try this for just one game. If you win, try it for one more.
* Your partner is hitting weak serves or return of serves.
* You are being targeted at the net.
* You are being passed down the line and you are forced to hug your alley.
* You are having a really bad day at the net.
* You need a change of strategy.

Deuce Again? Play Australian!!

Use the Australian doubles format (or the "I" formation) as a change of strategy when nothing else is working. Playing Australian will also:

* Take away your opponents' crosscourt weapon. Force the returner to hit to a different area. Some players do not know how to hit down the line.
* Cut off angles hit on the return of serve or hit during play.
* Protect your own weakness. Australian, played on the ad side, turns two exposed backhands into two forehands.
* Keep the net player aggressive. Australian, played on the ad side, will allow the net player to poach towards their forehand.

135

Defense Against Australian

In this order:

* Continue hitting *crosscourt* if the net player is weak.

* *Lob* a strong net player. The server must then change directions to retrieve your crosscourt lob.

* Hit *deep or low down the line*. Caution: Your opponents' strategy is to have you hit down the line. Don't immediately fall into their trap.

Should We Switch?

Returners: Consider switching sides of the court at the beginning of a new set if you lost badly (6-0, 6-1, 6-2.)

Do not change your receiving side if you lose a close 6-3, 6-4 or 7-5 set; or, of course, 7-6 (set score if a tiebreaker was played).

Servers: The most effective server should start serving a new set.

"Most effective" does not always mean "most powerful".

Trish and Paul were playing mixed doubles against two very strong, hard-hitting opponents. Trish had yet to return Mike's serve and had already been aced a number of times. Winning 6-5 in the third set, Trish knew they could take the match if they could find a way to break Mike's serve. As they changed sides of the court, Trish said, "You know Mike, you have the most incredible serve I have ever faced. Do you breathe in or out when you make contact with the ball?" "I don't know, I've never thought about it", Mike replied. Mike double faulted the next three points and Trish and Paul won the match...Is this cheating???

FOOTWORK

Split Step (Bunny Hop)
Just Before your ✪ Opponent Contacts the Ball

This allows you to:
* Maintain your balance and
  change direction easily.
* Stop.
* Step into the ball.

Step "Loudly" into Your Volley Like a Boxer Steps into His "Knock Out" Punch

Stepping "loudly" forces you to plant your foot and shift your weight forward:

* Step with the left foot for forehands.
* Step with the right foot for backhands.
* Step opposite if you are lefty.

Step forward, not sideways...and definitely not backwards, on all strokes.

Drag Your Back Toe

Forcing you to:

* **Step** into your groundstrokes and volleys.

* **Shift** your weight forward.

* **Stop** before you hit.

* **Rotate** your hips and upper body correctly.

* **Wear** out your shoes (sorry).

Quick Recovery with the Side Step

After running for a ball, face your opponent
as you shuffle sideways back to your position.

Center Mark

I didn't realize that watching the finals match for the high school regional championships in Alexandria, Virginia was going to be so entertaining. The tennis was great, but the officiating was hysterical. The linesmen were P.E. teachers from the area, some of whom had never even played tennis, let alone officiate a match. Most of the line calls were made properly, **when** they remembered to make them, **when** they remembered which lines they were supposed to call, and **when** they remembered they didn't have to yell "good" when the ball bounced in. However, the players and the audience doubled over when a linesman called a foot fault.....on the **return** of server. OOPS!

MENTAL TOUGHNESS

During a Point...
be Physically Tough and Mentally Alert

Between Points...
be Physically Relaxed and Mentally Tough

Mental Toughness Takes Practice!

Some people are gifted with the ability to concentrate under pressure.
Others, have to *learn* to become mentally tough!

Then, like everything else, it must be practiced.

Stay Confident & Stay Focused Between Points!!

Focus your eyes on your strings
to keep your concentration level at its highest...like the pros.

Whatever the score, stay confident
and keep stroking the ball like you know how.

A Note to Parents & Coaches

Pull your child off the court when he shows inappropriate behavior (yelling, cursing, throwing or hitting the racket on the ground, smashing the ball, cheating, or being extremely rude). Make him realize that it is unacceptable to act this way and he will not compete until he learns to control himself. Working with your child on appropriate behavior is more important than working on his strokes. Tennis is an extremely frustrating sport. If tempers are not controlled at a young age, the game will not be fun for him, his partner, his opponent, or you.

It's very difficult to play against yourself as well as an opponent.

For the fifth season in a row, my AA1 team was in the finals of the city playoffs. We anticipated another loss because we were facing the same team that had eliminated us in all the previous finals. Better to admit defeat: We all showed up wearing brown outfits with "we're number 2" written on our t-shirts. Guess what...we're still number 2.

TENNISELLANEOUS

Broken Strings ??

Don't panic, just see your local stringer. If it will be several days before you get your racket to your stringer, release its tension by clipping the center strings.

Tennis Elbow Problems ????

Practice correct form:

* Contact the ball early.

* Follow through "on edge".

* Pull the racket back with the shoulder, not the elbow, on a one-handed backhand.

OR check your equipment:

* Restring your racket at a low tension using thin gauge strings.

* Use a racket that has a flexible frame, and an open string pattern (farther apart).
  A redemption (staggered) string system may be very effective.

What's so Exciting about WORLD TEAMTENNIS?

* Play consists of one set of women's singles, women's doubles, men's singles, men's doubles, and mixed doubles.
* No-ad scoring. First team to get 4 points wins the game.
* A 9-point tiebreaker (first one to 5 points) is played at 5-5 in the set.
* Each game won is a point for that team.
* Players change sides every 4 games.
* Coaching is allowed between points, games, and sets.
* Substitutions are allowed at any time.
* **_Let serves are good!!_** (professional play only, and is this great to watch!)
* The fifth set is a come-from-behind set. If the fifth set is won by the trailing team and the trailing team is still behind in overall cumulative score, the match goes into WORLD TEAMTENNIS overtime. Overtime continues until the leading team wins one game (in which they win the match). If the score becomes tied, a "Super Tiebreaker" is played.

Call 1-800-TEAM TEN for info on Prince/WORLD TEAMTENNIS leagues in your area.

Traveling? Need a Match?

Try CompuServe! The Tennis Forum on CompuServe offers you a chance to speak with players of your level around the world. The next time you go out of town and need a game or find the best place to play, send a message with your NTRP rating to the over 3 million CompuServe members. If you have CompuServe, type "GO TENNIS". If you do not have CompuServe, call 1-800-524-3388 (ask for representative 631).

Consider how chaotic it is coaching a carefree group of kids whose names consist of Kelley, Kristin, Kaley, Kellyn, Courtney, and Katie. At Litchfield Hundred in Cobb County, Georgia, keeping these names consistently correct   is my concern. CONFUSING!! Also competing in this class are Erin, Lindsey and Jessica....they are honorary members of the team.

The ☆One-Half Hour Lesson

A Prose for Tennis Pros

I want to work on only volleys today,
I need to learn how to put them away.
Because all I do is keep them in play,
I definitely want to work on my volleys today.

But maybe you should show me how to serve with some spin,
Even though I know I can get the ball in.
My service games, I rarely do win,
Yes, let us work on serving with spin.

But I do need to work on my backhand with you,
I still don't know whether to use one hand or two.
And where its heading I haven't a clue.
I really NEED to work on my backhand with you.

My forehand is really a weapon for me,
Even though I've lost it...temporarily.
If you feed me some balls I'm sure you will see,
That my forehand is truly a weapon for me.

So, let's go over volleys, serves, backhands and forehands,
Yes, let's even add some power...
And all this, I think to myself,
All of this, in just one half-hour.

by Paige O'Neill

A Note from the Author

Teaching proper strokes and strategies to students is easy. Having them remember and utilize these ideas in a match is not so easy! 'Tips & Tales of the Tennis Court' is a collection of my favorite tennis tips that I have accumulated throughout my 12 years of instructing. They are designed to be easy to read, easy to understand, **and** extremely easy to remember. I hope you enjoy reading this book and may all your balls go **in**!!

TELEPHONE ORDERS: 1-770-578-1639
TO FAX IN YOUR ORDER: 1-770-578-0083

SEND MAIL ORDERS TO: **TIPS & TALES**
2100 ROSWELL ROAD
SUITE 200C-223
MARIETTA, GA 30062

ONLY $12.95

Please send _____ (#copies) of "Tips & Tales of the Tennis Court."
I understand that I may return any book(s) for a full refund for any reason.

PLEASE SHIP TO:

NAME _____

ADDRESS _____

_____

CITY _____ **ST** _____ **ZIP** _____

SHIPPING INSTRUCTIONS:	
_____#COPIES @ $12.95 = SUBTOTAL	
5% SALES TAX *(GEORGIA RESIDENTS ONLY)*	
SHIPPING (BOOK RATE): *$2.00 FOR THE FIRST BOOK* *$0.75 FOR EACH ADDITIONAL BOOK.*	
TOTAL ENCLOSED	**$**
PAYMENT METHOD: ☐ Check ☐ Money Order ☐ C.O.D. *MAKE CHECKS PAYABLE TO: TIPS & TALES*